CORNISH GRAMMAR

by JOHN PAGE

Bard of the Cornish Gorsedd

'Gwas Kenethlow'

Kesva an Taves Kernewek ~ the Cornish Language Board

First edition 1977
Second edition 1982
Third edition 1988
Fourth (revised) edition, October1993
(reprinted April 1994 and January 1996)

Fifth (amended) edition, September 2008

An lyver ma yw profys dhe Wella Brown
neb re wrug meur yn unn dhyski
agan yeth ni dhe'n werin.

ISBN 978-1-902917-82-5

RAGLAVAR

The first edition of this book, under the title *'Grammar for the Second and Third Grades'*, was published privately by the author in 1977.

The author's preface to the second edition (Kowethas an Yeth Kernewek 1982) states:

"This book contains all the points of grammar required from students attempting the second grade of the Cornish Language Board's examination, arranged in the order of the Board's syllabus.

"In addition the grammar required for the third, advanced, grade is reviewed. There follows a succinct summary of the verb **bos**, *'to be'."*

A third edition was published by the Cornish Language Board (Kesva an Taves Kernewek) in 1988, editor Dr Ken George. The editor's preface to that third edition states:

"John Page, the author of this work, was an interpreter by profession, and a grammarian of the old school. Upon retirement, he added Cornish to his impressive list of languages, and having passed all three grades in one year, began to teach it in Truro. He was for a time the General Secretary of the Cornish Language Board. Although he left Cornwall for some years to travel on the continent, he returned, and ran an active class in Luxulyan up to the time of his death in 1984.

"In this edition the amended spelling system is used. The text has been slightly revised by the editor; in particular references to word order have been clarified, and a new section on the negative particles included. References to page numbers in P.A.S. Pool's 'Cornish for Beginners' have been omitted.

"The re-organisation of the Board's examination system has necessitated a change of title. The layout and character of the book have not been changed, however: there are still three chapters— Grammar for the Third Grade (formerly 2nd grade), Grammar for the Fourth Grade (formerly 3rd grade), and the Verb **Bos**."

Preface to the fourth edition: the adoption of Kernewek Kemmyn by the Cornish Language Board and the publication of the second edition of *'A Grammar of Modern Cornish'* by Wella Brown (Cornish Language Board 1993) and the *'Gerlyver Kernewek Kemmyn'* by Dr Ken George (Cornish Language Board 1993) have necessitated some minor changes to John Page's well-tested work. These two works are essential reference books for advanced students.

CONTENTS

A. GRAMMAR FOR THE THIRD GRADE

I ADVERBS

Adverbs are normally formed from adjectives by prefixing **yn**[5]:

da	good	**yn ta**	well
lowen	happy	**yn lowen**	happily
gwir	true	**yn hwir**	truly
men	strong	**yn fen**	strongly

In other words, **yn** corresponds with English *-ly*.

II INFINITIVES WITH 'YN UNN'

As we have seen, the present participle is formed by prefixing **ow**[4] or **owth** to the infinitive of the verb. However, when the participle modifies a preceding verb, we use the particle **yn unn**[2]:

ev a wrug dos yn unn boenya
he came running. (i.e. 'in a run')

Here *'running'* describes *how* he came - it modifies the verb *'came'* hence the **yn unn** form is used.

ev a grias ughel y lev yn unn leverel ...
he cried aloud saying ...
ev a dheuth yn unn waytya ow gweles
he came hoping to see me

III PRESENT PARTICPLE WITH 'ORTH'

When the present participle has a pronoun object, **ow** or **owth** becomes **orth** and the pronoun is a possessive. The mutation of the infinitive will depend on the mutation required by the possessive:

orth ow hommendya	*introducing me*
orth y weles	*seeing him*
orth agan klywes	*hearing us*
orth hy threghi	*cutting it* (f)

IV COMPARISON OF ADJECTIVES AND ADVERBS

Adjectives are made comparative (English -*er*) by adding **a**; the final consonant is doubled, and (if appropriate) hardened, and the preceding vowel is short:

bras [‘bra:s] *big*	**brassa** [‘brassa] *bigger*	**an brassa** *biggest*
teg [‘tE:g] *fine*	**tekka** [‘tekka] *finer*	**an tekka** *finest*
koth [‘ko:θ] *old*	**kottha** [‘koθθa] *older*	**an kottha** *oldest*

Note above that when **th** is doubled it is spelled **tth**.

Four common adjectives compare irregularly:

byghan *small*		**le** *smaller*		**an lyha** *smallest*
meur *much*		**moy** *more*		**an moyha** *most*
da *good*		**gwell** *better*		**an gwella** *best*
drog *bad*		**gweth** *worse*		**an gwettha** *worst*
	or	**lakka**	or	**an lakka**

Polysyllables may, and past participles must, form the comparative with **moy**:

konnyk	**moy konnyk**	**an moyha konnyk**
clever	*cleverer*	*cleverest*

Comparative and superlative adjectives may follow their nouns, in which case the normal rules of mutation apply:

benyn deg	**benyn dekka**
a pretty woman	*a prettier woman*

but they often come before their nouns, in which case mutation does not occur:

tekka benyn	**an tekka benyn**
a prettier woman	*the prettiest woman*

The superlative may come either before or after the noun; if it comes after a feminine singular noun (or a masculine plural noun denoting persons) it is liable to second state mutation:

an gwella fordh or **an fordh wella** *the best road*;

When the comparative is formed with **moy**, it will follow the noun, but there will be no mutation, since the adjective is separated from the noun:

an venyn gonnyk	*the clever woman*
an venyn moy konnyk	*the cleverer woman*

'Than' in comparisons is **ages** (can be shortened to **es**):

Yowann yw kottha ages Peder
John is older than Peter
Yowann yw moy konnyk ages y vroder
John is cleverer than his brother

Ages combines with personal pronouns:

agesov vy	*than I*	**ageson ni**	*than we*
agesos jy	*than you* (s.)	**agesowgh hwi**	*than you* (p)
agesso ev	*than he*	**agessa i**	*than they*
agessi hi	*than she*		

gwell yw ev agesos jy.	*he is better than you.*

In equative comparisons *(as ... as ...)* we use:

mar[2] ...**avel** ... or **maga**[5] ... **avel** ...:

mar verr avel Yowann	**maga ta avel owr**
as short as John	*as good as gold*

Avel also combines with the pronouns:

avelov vy	*as I*	**avelon ni**	*as we*
avelos jy	*as you* (s)	**avelowgh hwi**	*as you* (p)
avello ev	*as he*	**avella i**	*as they*
avelli hi	*as she*		

mar vras avelli hi	**maga koth avella i**
as big as she (is)	*as old as they (are)*

However, when the comparison is with a verb rather than a noun or pronoun, the **avel** becomes **dell**, and there is a State 2 mutation:

mar dha dell allav	**maga teg dell welydh**
as well as I can	*as pretty as you can see*

Comparison of adverbs is normally expressed by using the comparative form of the adjective:

ev a vyw lowenna lemmyn
he lives more happily now
ev a skrif gwell es dell wrav
he writes better than I do

V INFIXED PRONOUNS

When a pronoun is the object of a simple tense of a verb (i.e. not compounded with one of the auxiliaries), the object is infixed between the particle and the verb. Apostrophes are used to mark these infixed pronouns, which are:

‘m	*me*	**‘gan**	*us*	(rarely **‘n**)
‘th[5]	*you* (s)	**‘gas**	*you* (p)	(rarely **‘s**)
‘n	*him/it*	**‘s**	*them*	
‘s	*her/it*			

The infixed pronouns prevent mutation of the verb by the preceding particle. The only one of them to cause mutation itself is **‘th**, which requires a modified form of State 5.

ev a’th kara meur	**my a’n gorras y’n amari**
he loved you much	*I put it* (m) *in the cupboard*

The following example is to be regarded as poetic:

A’s gwelsys ? Na’s gwelis	*Have you seen her ? No*
Ny’s gwelis	*I haven’t seen her*

Note that in the compound tenses with the auxiliaries, the possessive form of the pronoun is used:

my a*’n* gorras y’n amari *but* **my a wrug *y* worra y’n amari**
Yowann a*’s* gwelas *but* **Yowann a wrug *hy* gweles**

VI THE FUTURE TENSE OF ‘BOS’

bydhav	*I shall be*	**bydhyn**	*we shall be*
bydhydh	*you* (s) *will be*	**bydhowgh**	*you* (p) *will be*
bydh	*he, she, it will be*	**bydhons**	*they will be*

The mutations undergone are: State 2 **B** > **V**; State 5 **B** > **F**.

When the subject precedes the verb, the particle is **a**^{2}. When the complement precedes the verb, there is no particle, but State 2 mutation remains. When the verb comes before the subject and the complement, the particle is **y**^{5}. In questions the particle is **a**^{2}:

an fleghes a vydh lowen hedhyw
the children will be happy today
lowen vydh an fleghes hedhyw
the children will be happy today
hedhyw y fydhons i lowen
today they will be happy
a vydhons i lowen ?
will they be happy ?
a ny vydh an fleghes lowen ?
won't the children be happy ?

VII REFLEXIVE VERBS

Verbs are made reflexive by prefixing **om-**^{2}:

golghi	*to wash*	**omwolghi**	*to wash oneself*

res yw dhymm golghi an dillas
I must wash the clothes
res yw dhymm omwolghi
I must wash myself

There is sometimes a small change of meaning when a verb is made reflexive:

gul	*to make*	**omwul**	*to pretend*
kemmeres	*to take*	**omgemmeres**	*to undertake*

VIII ADVERBIAL NUMBERS

Adverbial numbers are formed with the word **gweyth** *'occasion'* which takes the feminine form of the number and is mutated if appropriate:

unnweyth *once* — **diwweyth** *twice*
teyrgweyth *three times* — **pedergweyth** *four times*
kankweyth *one hundred times* — **milweyth** *one thousand times*

my a wrug y elwel teyrgweyth *I called him three times*
ny allav vy y wul diwweyth *I can't do it twice*

The call of the Gorsedd is:

Unnweyth orthowgh y hwovynnav, eus kres ?
Diwweyth orthowgh y hwovynnav, eus kres ?
Teyrgweyth orthowgh y hwovynnav, eus kres ?

IX INDIRECT STATEMENT

A detailed explanation of this is to be found in *A Grammar of Modern Cornish* (§334-8). It is convenient to tabulate the rules:

1) Affirmative statement with *pronoun* subject involving the present or imperfect of **bos**. Use a possessive pronoun and the infinitive:

ev a leveris *y vos* klav
he said that he is/was ill
my a vynn *agas bos* omma
I wish you were here
ny vynnyn ni *aga bos* ledhys
we don't want them to be killed

2) Affirmative statement with noun subject involving the present or imperfect of **bos**. The noun and any adjectives follow **bos** in the infinitive:

ev a lever *bos Yowann* omma
he says that John is here
hi a vynna *bos lowen hy mab*
she wanted her son to be happy
my a dyb *bos Tamsin* pur deg
I think that Tamsin is very pretty

3) Affirmative statement with any subject, any other tense of **bos**, or any other verb. Use the *'subject'* + *'dhe'* + *'infinitive'* construction:

hi a lever *ev dhe dhos*
she says that he is coming/will come
ev a dyb *ni dhe vos* ena
he thinks that we were/are/shall be there

4) For affirmative indirect statements, there is another method, using the **y**[5] particle:

ev a grys *y fydhav* ena
he believes that I shall be there
ev a wayt *y teu* Yowann
he hopes that John will come

5) When the statement is negative, other rules apply. In negative indirect statements, we use the particle **na**[2]. If the subject is a noun, then the verb will be in the 3rd person singular, but if it is a pronoun, then the verb must agree with its subject:

an den a leveris *nag esa* avalow y'n varghas
the man said that there were no apples in the market
ow thas a leveris *nag esens* i ena

my father said that they weren't there
ev a grys *na vynn* an fleghes dos
he believes that the children don't want to come
ev a leveris *na yllyn* y wul
he said that I couldn't do it

In 1), 2) and 3), the relative time of the occurrence is supplied by the context.

Now consider these two examples:

My a grys aga bos da
I believe that they are good
My a grys nag yns i da
I believe they are not good

The first is affirmative, so we apply Rule 1. The second is negative, so we apply Rule 5.

Now note:

Ny grysav aga bos da
I do not believe that they are good

Although the introducing verb *(I do not believe)* is negative, the statement is affirmative, so Rule 1 applies.

These five rules are very important and are fundamental to all good Cornish composition. They should be thoroughly mastered.

X THE PAST PARTICIPLE

Almost all past participles end in **-ys**:

gweles	*to see*	**gwelys**	*seen*
kara	*to love*	**kerys**	*loved*
leverel	*to say*	**leverys**	*said*

Verbs ending in **-ya** had [-jIs] in Middle Cornish, variously spelled *-yys*, *-yes*, *-ijs*, but this was simplified to [-Is], and it is convenient to adopt this simplification:

redya	*to read*	**redys**	*read*

Verbs in **-he** from adjectives have their past participle in **-hes**:

glanhe	*to clean*	**glanhes**	*cleaned*
toemmhe	*to warm*	**toemmhes**	*warmed*

There are a few noticeably irregular formations:

gul	*to do, make*	**gwrys**	*done, made*
mos	*to go*	**gyllys**	*gone*
dos	*to come*	**devedhys**	*come*
ri	*to give*	**res**	*given*
doen	*to carry*	**degys**	*carried*

The main function of the past participle is to form the passive voice with **bos**:

Yowann a skrif lyther
John writes a letter
an lyther a veu skrifys gans Yowann
the letter was written by John

The past participle also makes for elegant semi-poetic usage:

ha devedhys an gorthugher
when the evening was come
gyllys an eledh arta dhe nev
when the angels had gone again to heaven
koen dybrys, koska a wrug ev
having supped, he slept
an ober kowlwrys, y tegemmersons aga gober
the work completed, they received their wages

XI THE IMPERSONAL ENDING

In addition to the six personal endings of verbs, Cornish has a seventh, referring to an indefinite person (like *'one'* in English). In principle this exists in all tenses, but in practice it is found mainly in the present tenses, both indicative (regular ending **-ir**) and subjunctive (ending **-er**):

dell welir
as is seen/as one sees
yndella y skrifir
thus it is written
lev an gog a glywir y'n tir
the voice of the cuckoo is heard in the land
rag gwitha kres y hwrer hemma
to preserve peace one does this
henn a gevir yn oberow Mordon
that is found in Mordon's work

It is to be noted that all of the last three examples could have been expressed using **bos** and the past participle (i.e. the passive voice):

lev an gog yw klywys y'n tir

rag gwitha kres yth yw gwrys hemma
henn yw kevys yn oberow Mordon

A good example with the present subjunctive is found in the Gorsedd ceremony:

Dhe Gernow, Kernyas, hwyth dha gorn, may'n klywer yn hy feswar sorn
To Cornwall, Horner, blow your horn, that it may be heard in her four corners

XII PREPOSITIONS

Of the prepositions which are conjugated, the eight commonest have been dealt with in *Cornish Grammar for Beginners*, section XIX. To these may be added **a-rag**, which conjugates like **rag**, and means *'before',* but only of place and not of time:

ev a sevis a-rag Yowann
he stood before (in front of) John
but **ev a dheuth kyns Yowann**
he came before John (did)

Another class of prepositions includes **erbynn** *(against),* **war-lergh** *(after)* and **yn kever** *(regarding)*. These are separable when used with pronouns, but inseparable when used with nouns. When separated, they observe the mutational rules of the pronoun concerned:

erbynn an fos	**er ow fynn**
against the wall	*against me*
war-lergh an den	**war y lergh**
after the man	*after him*
yn kever an dra	**yn y gever**
about the matter	*about (regarding) him*

Erbynn may also be used to convey the meaning *'to meet',* either as a separated preposition:

ev a dheuth er aga fynn
he met them (came against them)

or as part of a verb:

ev a's dyerbynnas *he met them*

XIII INTERROGATIVES

For the most part, these have been dealt with in Grammar for the First Grade, but there was one important omission: **prag**, *'why'*. The reason for this is that all questions asked with *'why'* require the answer *'because'*, and this involves a construction not dealt with until the next section. In the meantime, we may observe that **prag**, alone among the interrogatives, requires the particle **y⁵**:

prag y fynn'ta y brena ?
why do you want to buy it ?
prag yth esowgh hwi ow poenya ?
why are you running ?
prag yth oel Tamsin mar ahwer ?
why is Tamsin crying so bitterly ?

As you see, none of these can be answered without the conjunction *'because';* see section XIV below.

In the negative, the interrogative *'why not'* is **prag na²**:

prag na vynn'ta y brena ?
why don't you want to buy it ?
prag nag esos ta ow poenya ?
why aren't you running ?
prag na oel Tamsin lemmyn ?
why isn't Tamsin crying now ?

XIV CONJUNCTIONS

These are conveniently discussed in two groups:

Group 1: requiring infinitive construction

awos, **drefenn**, **rag**	*because*
kyns	*before*
wosa	*after*

The rules for these are similar to the rules for indirect statement, and need not be repeated. Here are some illustrative examples:

awos y vos myghtern
because he is/was a king
awos bos Arthur myghtern
because Arthur is/was a king
drefenn ow bos re goth
because I am/was too old
kyns bos Yowann kottha
before John is/was older
wosa ev dhe dhybri
after he eats or *has/had eaten*

As the infinitive of the verb is used, there is no indication of time, and this must be supplied by the context.

We now find that we can answer the six questions asked with **prag** and **prag na** in the previous section:

awos bos edhomm dhymm anodho
because I need it

awos agan bos diwedhes
because we are late

drefenn hi dhe gelli hy mamm
because she has lost her mother

drefenn y vos re gostek
because it is too expensive

rag ow bos skwith
because I am tired

rag hi dhe gavoes hy mamm
because she has found her mother

Group 2: conjunctions followed by a conjugated verb

pan^{2}	*when*
dell^{2}	*as*
kettell^{2}	*as soon as*
fatell^{2}	*how*
erna^{2}	*until*
nammna^{2}	*nearly, almost*
mar^{4}	*if*
may^{5}	*so that*
kyn^{5}	*although*

May and **kyn** become **mayth** and **kynth** before vowels and radical '**h**' in all verbs; **erna**, **nammna** and **mar** become **ernag**, **nammnag** and **mars** before vowels only in **bos** and **mos**.

Conjunctions in this group must be followed directly by the verb, without any intervening word or particle. However, when the conjunction ends in a consonant and the verb has an infixed object, **y** is inserted for euphony.

The negatives used are:

pan na²
kyn na²
ma na²
mar ny²

Note that in the negative, **may** has become **ma**, and that **mar** is the odd man out, requiring **ny** and not **na**.

Some illustrative examples should make all of this clear:

pan dheu gwav	*when winter comes*
pan y'm gwelas	*when he saw me*
dell lever Yowann	*as John says*
kettell glywsyn ni	*as soon as we heard*
fatell allav vy ?	*how can I ?*
erna dheu an medhek	*until the doctor comes*
nammna wrug vy merwel	*I nearly died*
mar teu Yowann	*if John comes*
mars yw teg an gewer	*if the weather is fine*
may koedhas ev	*so that he fell*
kyn teuth an medhek	*though the doctor came*
pan na dheuth Yowann	*when John didn't come*
ma na dheuth Yowann	*so that John didn't come*
mar ny dheu Yowann	*if John doesn't come*

Awos *'because'* in Group 1 cannot be used in the negative, and in its place are used either **drefenn na** or **rag na**:

prag na wrons i dybri ?
why don't they eat ?

rag nag eus nown dhedha
because they are not hungry

prag na dheu ev hedhyw ?
why doesn't he come today ?

drefenn na vynn ev gweles y vroder
because he doesn't want to see his brother

XV RELATIVE CLAUSES

This is discussed in detail in *A Grammar of Modern Cornish* (§340-3) but a little clarification is still desirable.

A typical relative clause is seen in the sentence : *'The man who wrote the book is a bard.'* Here the main sentence is *'The man is a bard',* and the relative clause is *'who wrote the book',* and is descriptive of *'man'.*

The relative particle is **a**[2]:

An den a skrifas an lyver yw bardh

We can also, if we wish, insert **neb** *'who'* in the sentence. There is no grammatical necessity to do so, but it may assist clarity:

An den neb a skrifas an lyver yw bardh

We can also use **hag** for this purpose, but usually of things rather than persons. **Hag** can be used for either things or persons, but **neb** only for persons:

an menhir (hag) a sev y'n garth yw pur goth
the stone which stands in the yard is very old

When the present tense of **bos** is involved, the form used is **eus** for indefinite subjects, and **usi** for definite subjects:

an lyver usi war an voes yw dhymm
the book which is on the table is mine

tus neb eus y'n chi
folk who are in the house

'I who', 'he who' are translated by **my neb**, **ev neb**, etc.:

my neb a gews orthis
I who am speaking to you

ni neb a wra merwel
we who are about to die

'That which' is translated by **an pyth**:

an pyth a syw	*that which follows*
an pyth esa y'n chi	*that which was in the house*

In the perfect tense, the particle is **re**^{2}:

an den re welis diwweyth yw devedhys
the man (whom) I have seen twice is come

an hwedhel re skrifsowgh hwi yw da
the story which you have written is good

In negative relative clauses, the particle is **na**^{2}:

an den neb na red ny woer travyth
the man who doesn't read knows nothing

an ger na glywsewgh hwi o dhe les
the word you hadn't heard was important

XVI PRESENT, IMPERFECT, PRETERITE AND PLUPERFECT TENSES

The endings in these tenses are regular, but the stems are liable to change, and need study.

The present tense needs no explanation. It deals with what is happening now, 'at this moment in time'. But since there is no separate future tense in Cornish (except in **bos** and one or two other verbs), the present tense may have a future meaning:

my a wel Yowann a-vorow
I see John tomorrow

The fact that we have added **a-vorow** gives contextual future meaning to the present **a wel**. However the more usual way of giving a future meaning is to use the present tense of the auxiliary verb **gul**:

my a wra gweles Yowann a-vorow

The imperfect tense requires rather more consideration, since it does not exist in English as a separate tense, but is expressed by the periphrasis *'was ----ing'*. In Cornish, however (and indeed in most other European languages), it does exist, and therefore needs to be understood and used properly.

The imperfect deals with continuing action in past time, as opposed to the preterite, which deals with a completed action. In English this can be expressed only as:

I was doing (imperfect) and *I did* (preterite)

but in Cornish we have the forms:

my a wre *I was doing* and **my a wrug** *I did*

Consider:

a wrens i redya lyver ? (imperfect)
were they reading a book ?

a wrussons i redya lyver (preterite)
did they read a book ?

We need to be particularly careful when using the verb *'to be',* as in English both imperfect and preterite are *'was',* but in Cornish we have:

o **esa** (imperfect)
a veu (preterite)

Consider the statement:

the bards were gathered together

This could mean either that the Bards were there in their circle, or that the Grand Bard had performed the act of calling them together.

In Cornish the first would be: **an Verdh o kuntellys warbarth**

and the second: **an Verdh a veu kuntellys warbarth**

The pluperfect tense in English is expressed as *'I had done'* -- more past than the perfect, hence the name *'pluperfect'*.

In Cornish, this tense is formed by prefixing **re**[2] to the conditional form, which has the endings:
-sen, **-ses**, **-sa**; **-sen**, **-sewgh**, **-sens**:

an den na re glywsa meur a hwedhlow
that man had heard many stories

ev a leveris re gavsa ev y lyver
he said that he had found his book

The conditional tense of **bos** is: **bien, bies, bia, bien, biewgh, biens**, and this also accepts the pluperfect particle **re**, but is not mutated by it:

my re bia y'n chi na
I had been in that house

an dus re bia ledhys gans eskerens
the people had been killed by enemies

The **re** particle cannot be used either in the interrogative or in the negative, and in such cases the precise meaning will have to be derived from the context.

B. GRAMMAR FOR THE FOURTH GRADE

Grammar for the Fourth Grade means in effect all the grammar that there is! When the second edition of this book was published (1982), grammar for the then Third Grade meant the summa of *Cornish Simplified* and its four supplements. Since then, the supplements have been published as a separate volume *(Cornish Simplified, vol. 2),* but more importantly, Wella Brown's definitive work *A Grammar of Modern Cornish* has appeared and is now published in its third, revised, edition.

P.A.S. Pool's *Cornish for Beginners* covers all the grammar required for Grade 3 but only some of that for Grade 4. The advanced student is therefore strongly advised to study Wella Brown's grammar. This book and its precursor Grammar for the

First Grade and the Auxiliary Verbs are not in themselves enough. They are not intended as a substitute for the works just mentioned, but as a guide to them, presenting the various points of grammar in the order of the Board's syllabus, and introducing the student to the grammar progressively.

1 THE VERB 'A'M BEUS'

Far from being difficult, **a'm beus** is a very easy verb to use. Note that the verb has differing forms for *'he'* and *'she',* and that the latter are identical with the forms for *'they';*

		present tense *I have*	imperfect tense *I was having*
S	1	**a'm beus**	**a'm bo**
	2	**a'th eus**	**a'th o**
	3m	**a'n jeves**	**a'n jevo**
	3f	**a's teves**	**a's tevo**
P	1	**a'gan beus**	**a'gan bo**
	2	**a'gas beus**	**a'gas bo**
	3	**a's teves**	**a's tevo**

		preterite tense *I had*	future tense *I shall have*
S	1	**a'm beu**	**a'm bydh**
	2	**a'feu**	**a'fydh**
	3m	**a'n jeva**	**a'n jevydh**
	3f	**a's teva**	**a's tevydh**
P	1	**a'gan beu**	**a'gan bydh**
	2	**a'gas beu**	**a'gas bydh**
	3	**a's teva**	**a's tevydh**

		conditional tense *I should have*	past habitual tense *I used to have*
S	1	**a'm bia**	**a'm bedha**
	2	**a'fia**	**a'fedha**
	3m	**a'n jevia**	**a'n jevedha**
	3f	**a's tevia**	**a's tevedha**
P	1	**a'gan bia**	**a'gan bedha**
	2	**a'gas bia**	**a'gas bedha**
	3	**a's tevia**	**a's tevedha**

		present subjunctive *I may have*	imperfect subjunctive *I might have*
S	1	**a'm bo**	**a'm be**
	2	**a'fo**	**a'fe**
	3m	**a'n jeffo**	**a'n jeffa**
	3f	**a's teffo**	**a's teffa**
P	1	**a'gan bo**	**a'gan be**
	2	**a'gas bo**	**a'gas be**
	3	**a's teffo**	**a's teffa**

Quite simply, the verb a'm beus means *'have'*. So far, the only way we have learned to express this has been to use the idioms **yma gans** and **yma dhe**:

yma genev pluvenn	*I have a pen*
eus kath dhis ?	*have you got a cat ?*
yma nown dhedha	*they are hungry*

Unlike all other Cornish verbs, **a'm beus** goes into the proper person and number when preceded by a pronoun subject:

my a'm beus pluvenn	*I have a pen*
i a's tevo lyvrow	*they had books*

It is clear from the twenty examples quoted by Caradar in his *Cornish Simplified* that the possession indicated by **a'm beus** can be either material or abstract, and that it can extend to the needs and emotions:

an tiek a'n jeves kans davas
the farmer has a hundred sheep

hwi a'gas beus an galloes dh'y wul
you have the power to do it

hi a's teves nown	**ni a'gan bo own**
she is hungry	*we were afraid*

ev a'n jevedha koffi dh'y hansel ev
he was in the habit of having coffee for his breakfast

i a's tevydh sowdhan
they will have a big surprise

A'm beus cannot be used interrogatively (except using the positive form with rising intonation, and with certain interrogative pronouns and adverbs), and questions regarding possession are therefore usually asked using **eus gans ?** or **eus dhe ?**:

eus chi dhodho yn Kernow ?
has he a house in Cornwall ?
eus, chi bras a'n jeves yn Kammbronn
yes, he has a big house in Camborne

A'm beus can be used negatively, both in direct and indirect clauses, the particles being **ny** and **na** respectively:

ny'n jeves ki	**ev a lever na'n jeves ki**

he hasn't a dog	*he says he hasn't a dog*

When the verb is used negatively before a verbal noun (infinitive verb), it acquires the meaning *'cannot':*

ny'm beus lyver	**ny'm beus kana**
I haven't a book	*I am unable to sing*

The rules for the use of **y** and **a** particles are identical to those for other verbs:

(a) when the subject or the object starts, the particle is **a**;
(b) when anything other than the subject or object starts (viz. an adverb or adverbial clause), the particle is **y**:

my a'm beus chi	(subject starts)
chi a'm beus	(object starts)
yn Truru y'm beus chi	(adverbial phrase starts)

The particle **re** can be prefixed to the preterite to obtain perfect meaning, and to the conditional to obtain pluperfect meaning:

i a's teva kinyow da	**i re's teva kinyow da**
they had a good dinner	*they have had a good dinner*
hi a's tevia skruth	**hi re's tevia skruth**
she would have a shock	*she had had a shock*

II THE SUBJUNCTIVE MOOD

It is sometimes difficult for English speakers to understand this mood of the verb as it has almost disappeared from English. However we still do (or ought to) say :

if I were ...	*if it be so ...*

The subjunctive mood is discussed fully by Wella Brown in *A Grammar of Modern Cornish* (§229). There are six main uses of the subjunctive, and as the Fourth Grade student will undoubtedly be studying *A Grammar of Modern Cornish*, all that is necessary here is to recapitulate and to give a few modern examples.

(1) The present subjunctive prefixed with the particle **re**[2] expresses a wish:

re bo lowena dhis !	*may you be happy !*
re dheffo an jydh !	*may the day come !*
re's teffo kres !	*may they have peace !*

(2) The present subjunctive expresses the indefinite future after such conjunctions as **pan** *'when'*, **erna** *'until'*, **kyn** *'although'*:

pan vo omma
when he is/may be/will be here
erna vo kowlwrys an ober
until the work be done
kyn teffons i nosweyth
though they may come by night

This use of the subjunctive is found in two places in Boson's ***Yowann Chi an Hordh***:

en chei lebma vo dean koath ... (Boson's spelling)
yn chi le may fo den koth ...
in a house where there may be an old man ...

po chee & tha wreag an moiha looan varbarr
pan vo ty ha'th wreg an moyha lowen warbarth
when you and your wife will be most happy together

(3) The subjunctive is used with generalities such as *'whoever', 'wherever',* etc.:

piwpynag a vynno mos tre
whoever wants to go home
an re a dheffo hedhyw
those who may come today
le mayth yllyn
wherever we (may) go

(4) The subjunctive is used after superlatives:

ev a skrif gwella gallo
he writes the best he can
dos a wrav skonna gylliv
I shall come the soonest possible

Note that in such cases the verb appears in its radical unmutated form.

(5) When **may** *'so that'* is used to express purpose, the subjunctive must be used, either the present or the imperfect depending on the tense of the leading verb:

ev a'n gwra may hyllyn konvedhes
he does it so that we may understand

ev a'n gwrug may hallen konvedhes
he did it so that we might understand

But when **may** is used to express result, the indicative is used:

mar yeyn o hi may rewas an mor
it was so cold that the sea froze

(6) The subjunctive is used after *pray*, *command*, *take care*:

i a bys may fo sewen
they pray that it will be successful

ev a erghis dhymm mayth ellen
he ordered me to go

kemmer with may fo gwrys yn ta
take care that it be done well

However, in ***Yowann Chi an Hordh*** Boson wrote:

komeer weeth na reo gara an vorr goeth ...
kemmer with na wrewgh gasa an fordh goth ...
take care that you don't leave the old road ...

He has used the indicative **wrewgh** and not the subjunctive, which would be **wrellowgh**. Assuming that the choice was still open to him (i.e. that the subjunctive of **gul** was still current at the time of writing), one may suppose that the indicative was used because the farmer definitely knew that John was undertaking a journey where there would definitely be a choice of road. In an indefinite situation, the subjunctive would be used:

kemmerewgh with na wryllowgh goslowes orth gowyow
take care that you do not listen to lies

(7) There is a seventh very important use of the subjunctive which Smith does not mention in his Lesson 36, but refers to it in paragraph 2 of Appendix C on page 86, and that is its use after the suppositional *if*.

Mar[4] *'if'* introduces suppositions which could be, even certainly are, possible, in which case the indicative is used:

my a'n gwra mar kallav
I'll do it if I can (probably can)

mars usi ena y hyllyn y weles
if he's there we can see him (probably is)

But when **mar** is used to introduce a supposition which is unlikely, or is definitely not the case, then the subjunctive must be used:

mar pe gwell an gewer, y hwrussen mos
if the weather were better, I would go

Here the inference is that the weather is bad, and the journey therefore unlikely; hence the conditional **y hwrussen mos** is used to show that the journey is conditional on the uncertain state of the weather.

Suppositions which are by definition impossible or inherently unlikely are introduced by **a**4 rather than by **mar**:

a kallen bywa bynitha !
if I could live for ever !

a pe omma dha das, ny wrusses yndella
if your father were here, you would not act thus

In the first case the supposition is impossible, and in the second it is clear that the father was not present.

III THE PARTICLES 'Y' AND 'YTH'

The subject of the **y**5 and **a**2 particles has already been covered in various paragraphs of this book and of *Grammar for the First Grade* (reference should also be made to *A Grammar of Modern Cornish)*, but it will do no harm to review the matter here.

The particles **y** and **yth** are used only in affirmative statements in which anything other than the subject or object begins the sentence:

y'n pras ryb an avon y hwelav bugh
in the meadow by the river I see a cow

lemmyn y klywav dha lev yn kler
now I hear your voice clearly

yn kler y klywav lemmyn dha lev
clearly now I hear your voice

Note that (except in the case of the long form of **bos** *'to be')*, and contrary to what has appeared in various text-books, a sentence begins with **y** + verb in exceptional circumstances only. The normal mode of expressing an affirmative statement is to use the nominal form:

my a glyw dha lev yn kler lemmyn
I hear your voice clearly now

Yth is used before vowels, and before **h** when the radical form of the verb begins with **h**, but when the initial **h** is the result of a mutation, the particle remains **y**:

lemmyn yth hanwav an skath ma *Ewyn an Mor*
I now name this boat Sea Spray

lemmyn y hallav dha weles
now I can see you

The **y** particle is used to introduce the verb in dependent clauses:

ev a leveris y klywsa ev an nowodhow da
he said that he had heard the good news

The **y** particle is used after conjunctions such as **pan** when there is an infixed pronoun object which would make the words unpronounceable:

pan y'n gwelav	*when I see him*

In the case of the verb **bos**, the forms **yma** and **ymons** are special cases, as they are deemed to contain the **y** particle integrally. These are the only two parts of **bos** which do incorporate the particle, and elsewhere it must be supplied. The **y** particle in **bos**, either implicit or explicit, is used in the same circumstances as with other verbs, with the proviso that in the present and imperfect tenses it may begin the sentence:

yma kath y'n lowarth	*there is a cat in the garden*
y'n lowarth yma kath	
yth esa kath y'n lowarth	*there was a cat in the garden*
y'n lowarth yth esa kath	

In all cases where the **y** particle is used, the subject will follow the verb, which must be conjugated to agree with a pronoun subject, but will remain in the 3rd singular for a noun subject (either singular or plural).

IV THE PARTICLE 'A'

The **a²** particle is used:

(1) To link the verb to the subject when this precedes the verb except in the tenses of **bos** and **mos** which begin with a vowel, in which case no particle is used:

an den a wel an pras
the man sees the meadow
an den a y'n pras
the man goes in the meadow

(2) When the object precedes the verb:

an pras a wel an den
the man sees the meadow

Note the following sentence is ambiguous:

an vugh a wel an den

It could mean *'the man sees the cow'* or *'the cow sees the man';* further information such as context is required to decide. Care should therefore be taken in using this relatively rare syntax.

(3) To introduce the verb in questions, except in the tenses of **bos** and **mos** which begin with a vowel, in which case no particle is used:

a wel an den an pras ?
does the man see the meadow ?

a an den y'n pras ?
does the man go in the field ?

(4) To introduce the verb in a relative clause:

yma an pras a wel an den yn Pennwydh
the field that the man sees is in Penwith

Again ambiguity may arise:

yma an vugh a wel an den yn Pennwydh
can mean *'the cow that the man sees is in Penwith'* or *'the cow that sees the man is in Penwith'*.

(5) As the object of an imperative when this has an infixed pronoun as its object:

a'n kemmer dhe-ves ha'y ladha
take him away and kill him

a'n glanhyn hedhyw
let us clean it today

When the **a** particle is used, the verb will agree with its subject when this follows the verb, again except in the case of plural nouns. When the subject precedes, the verb will remain in the 3rd person singular.

V THE NEGATIVE PARTICLES 'NY', 'NYNS', 'NA', 'NAG'

Ny and **nyns** are used in main clauses, **na** and **nag** are used in subordinate clauses.

Nyns and **nag** are used only with the tenses of **bos** and **mos** which begin with a vowel:

nyns esa denvyth a-ji
there was no-one inside

my a woer nag eth an tiek tre
I know that the farmer did not go home

Elsewhere, **ny** and **na** are used:

ny vynnens eva koffi
they would not drink coffee

tus a lever na woer ev redya
people say that he cannot read
As with the **y** particle, the subject follows the verb, which will be conjugated to agree with a pronoun subject, but remain in

the 3rd person singular for a noun subject (singular or plural).

When the negative particle is preceded by a plural noun, either in a main or a subordinate clause, the verb must still be conjugated:

an fleghes ny wrussons koska kyns deg eur de
the children did not sleep before ten o'clock yesterday

In this sentence, **an fleghes** is not the subject, and notwithstanding paragraphs 12 and 58 (2b) of *Cornish Simplified*, and page 10 of *Cornish for Beginners*, it is poor Cornish to use **ny wrug** instead of **ny wrussons**. The following example from ***Yowann Chi an Hordh***:

gor tero an dhiz rag riman a'ryg an bad-ober (Lhuyd)

was interpreted by Nance as (re-spelled):

gortewgh, a dus, rag an re ma ny wrug an bad-ober

which if correct, may be attributed to the influence of English. It would be interesting to hear of other examples from the texts of an apparent impersonal usage in a negative sentence with a plural subject. Such usage is abnormal (see para. 301 of *A Grammar of Modern Cornish)* and should be guarded against, especially in subordinate clauses such as:

ny wra vri orth an re na wodhons travyth yn kever Kernewek
he takes no notice of those who know nothing about Cornish

in which instead of the correct **na wodhons**, one often hears the erroneous **na woer**, or even worse, **ny woer**. This is a common mistake.

C THE VERB 'BOS'

The tenses of this irregular verb may be divided into two groups:

(a) the vowel tenses (present and imperfect, long and short forms);
(b) the b-tenses (a partly regular verb with the stem **bedh-**).

I VOWEL TENSES

		SHORT FORM present		LONG FORM present
S	1	**ov**	*I am*	**esov**
	2	**os**		**esos**
	3	**yw**		**yma/usi/eus**
P	1	**on**		**eson**
	2	**owgh**		**esowgh**
	3	**yns**		**ymons/esons**

Note: **yma** and **ymons** can only be used in the affirmative. In the negative, they are replaced by **nyns eus** or **nyns usi** and **nyns esons**. In the interrogative they are replaced by **eus** or **usi** and **esons**.

		SHORT FORM imperfect		LONG FORM imperfect
S	1	**en**	*I was*	**esen**
	2	**es**		**eses**
	3	**o**		**esa**

P	1	**en**	**esen**
	2	**ewgh**	**esewgh**
	3	**ens**	**esens**

Note: the potential ambiguity in the first person may be resolved by using the enclitics, e.g. **en vy** *'I was'*, **en ni** *'we were'*.

II B-TENSES

		future	imperfect habitual
S	1	**bydhav** *I shall be*	**bedhen** *I used to be*
	2	**bydhydh**	**bedhes**
	3	**bydh**	**bedha**
P	1	**bydhyn**	**bedhen**
	2	**bydhowgh**	**bedhewgh**
	3	**bydhons**	**bedhens**

		preterite	conditional
S	1	**beuv** *I was*	**bien** *I should be*
	2	**beus**	**bies**
	3	**beu**	**bia**
P	1	**beun**	**bien**
	2	**bewgh**	**biewgh**
	3	**bons**	**biens**

		present subjunctive	imperfect subjunctive
S	1	**biv** *I may be*	**ben** *I might be*
	2	**bi**	**bes**
	3	**bo**	**be**
P	1	**byn**	**ben**

	2	**bowgh**	**bewgh**
	3	**bons**	**bens**

imperative

S	1	---	
	2	**bydh**	*be* (s)
	3	**bedhes**	*let him/her/it be*
P	1	**bedhen**	*let us be*
	2	**bedhewgh**	*be* (p)
	3	**bedhens**	*let them be*

III THE COMPLEMENT

The verb *'to be'* does not have an object, but it must have a complement - a word or phrase which completes its meaning.

'He is' tells us next to nothing - we need to know who, what, where he is, what he is like or what he is doing.

Complements are of three main types:

(1) Descriptive - a noun or adjective describing the subject:

he is a man *she is old*

(2) Locative - locating the subject:

he is in the garden *the child is on the beach*

(3) Active - telling us what the subject is doing, usually with a present participle:

John is writing a letter *they are going to the pictures*

IV WORD ORDER

In English, the normal word order of the sentence is subject + verb + complement, as is seen above; but in Cornish this is by no means necessarily the case. The complement can, and often does, precede the subject.

We can say:

	an den yw koth	*the man is old*
or	**koth yw an den**	*old is the man*

The former order (subject + verb + complement) gives the emphasis to the *man*, i.e. *he* is old (the woman might not be), whilst the latter (complement + verb + subject) gives emphasis to the *oldness* - he is *old*, not young.

We can also, if we wish, use the **y** particle and start with the verb, though in all cases except the long forms of the vowel tenses, the verb would normally be precede by an adverb.

lemmyn yth yw an den na koth
now that man is old

V THE LONG AND SHORT FORMS OF THE VOWEL TENSES

In Cornish, there are two forms for the present and imperfect vowel tenses, the so-called 'long' and 'short' forms.

The 'short' form is used for complements of type 1 (descriptive), and the 'long' form is used for complements of types 2 and 3 (locative and active).

The 'long' form has a peculiarity in respect of the 3rd persons singular and plural **yma** and **ymons**. These are deemed to contain the **y** particle integrally, and therefore should be used only in sentences where the use of that particle would apply. In other words, they should not be preceded by the subject. **Yma** can have as its subject *'he', 'she' 'it'* or any noun, singular or plural. The subject of **ymons** (they) is incorporated in the verb, but may be emphasized by using the enclitic in the form **ymons i**:

yma an den y'n lowarth
the man is in the garden

yma den y'n lowarth
there is a man in the garden

It will be seen from the two examples above that when the subject is indefinite, **yma** will mean *'there is'*, but when it is definite, it will mean simply *'is'*.

Both of these could have been written the other way round:

y'n lowarth yma an den
y'n lowarth yma den

Placing the subject **den** before the location would be the answer to the question *'who is in the garden ?'*, while the other version would answer: *'where is the man ?'*

In negatives and interrogatives, **yma** is replaced by **nyns eus** and **eus** for indefinite subjects, and **nyns usi** and **usi** for definite subjects. **Ymons** is replaced by **nyns esons** and **esons** for both.

eus bara y'n chi ?	**eus**	**nag eus**
is there bread in the house ?	*yes*	*no*
usi dha vamm omma ?	**usi**	**nag usi**
is your mother here ?	*yes*	*no*

usi y vroder ow kwari peldroes hedhyw ?
is his brother playing football today ?

nyns eus keun owth hartha
there are no dogs barking

nyns usi an keun owth hartha
the dogs are not barking

ymons i ow neuvya y'n mor
they are swimming in the sea

esons i ow tos lemmyn ?	**esons**	**nag esons**
are they coming now ?	*yes*	*no*

There are no particular problems with the other persons of the present, or with any of the persons of the imperfect:

yth esov vy ow skrifa lyther
I am writing a letter

yth esen vy yn gweli ow koska
I was in bed sleeping

yth esa an fleghes y'n mor
the children were in the sea

It is to be noted that the **a** particle is not used with the vowel tenses.

VI MUTATION OF THE B-TENSES

These follow the usual rules of mutation:

State 2	**B**	>	**V**	after **a**, **ny**, **na**
State 4	**B**	>	**P**	after **mar** and **a** *'if'*, **ow** *'-ing'*
State 5	**B**	>	**F**	after **y**, **ple**, **p'eur**, **kyn**, **may**

except that the particle **re** does not mutate **B** to **V**.

When the complement precedes the verb, there is no **a** particle, but State 2 mutation remains as though there were:

lowen vydh Yowann	*John will be happy*
trist vydhons i	*they will be sad*

but if the subject had preceded, there would have been an **a** particle:

Yowann a vydh lowen
i a vydh trist

VII MODES OF EXPRESSION

When a pronoun subject, of whatever person or number, starts the sentence, the verb will always be in the 3rd person singular:

my yw skwith	*I am tired*
my o skwith	*I was tired*
my a vydh skwith	*I shall be tired*

When the sentence is negative, the pronoun cannot begin it, and the verb must agree with its subject:

nyns ov vy skwith	*I am not tired*
nyns en vy skwith	*I was not tired*
ny vydhav vy skwith	*I shall not be tired*

The same applies to interrogatives:

os ta skwith ?	*are you tired ?*
ens i skwith ?	*were they tired ?*
a ny vydhons i skwith ?	*won't they be tired ?*

A noun subject may begin a negative sentence:

an den nyns o skwith *the man was not tired*

but if it is a plural noun, then the verb must also be plural:

an fleghes nyns yns skwith *the children are not tired*

VIII USES OF TENSES

It is necessary to distinguish carefully between the imperfect and the preterite, both of which appear in English as *'I was',* etc. The imperfect deals with uncompleted or continuing action, while the preterite implies something done, finished:

the dog was lost

This could mean that you saw a lost dog trotting around, or that someone lost the dog. In Cornish the former would be:

	an ki o kellys	(imperfect)
and the latter:	**an ki a veu kellys**	(preterite)

The habitual imperfect deals with long-standing or usual situations in the past:

an ki a vedha kellys
the dog was habitually lost

an fer a vedha omma pub tri mis
the fair used to be here every three months

a vedhens i yn Breten Vyghan y'n hav ?
used they to be in Brittany in summer ?

The preterite can be made perfect by using **re** (no mutation with **bos**):

an ki re beu kellys
the dog has been lost

and the same particle converts the conditional to the pluperfect:

an ki re bia kellys
the dog had been lost

The imperative is used for commands:

bydh ena a-dro dhe hwegh eur
be there about six o'clock

bedhen fur
let us be wise

bedhens gelwys dhe'n demmedhyans
let them be invited to the wedding

The uses of the subjunctive are dealt with in the preceding section of this book, and a few examples will suffice:

re bo lowena dhis !	*may you be happy !*
pan vons i omma	*when they are here*
a pens i brassa !	*if only they were bigger !*
piwpynag a vo y'n chi	*whoever may be in the house*

a pe Yowann omma,	*if John were here,*
ev a wrussa kana	*he would sing*

IX IDIOMATIC USAGE

Finally, the use of **bos** with **gans** and **dhe** to convey the meaning *'have'*:

yma dhymm pluvenn	*I have (own) a pen*
yma genev pluvenn	*I have a pen (on me)*
yth esa nown dhedha	*they were hungry*
esa syghes dhedha?	*were they thirsty ?*
nyns esa hwans dhymm a vara	*I didn't want any bread*
eus edhomm dhis a dhowr ?	*do you need water ?*

With *'glad'* and *'sorry'* the short form of the vowel tenses is used:

da yw genev agas gweles hwi
I am happy to see you
drog yw gansa na wrussys dos
they are sorry that you didn't come

Using the comparative **gwell** and the conditional tense, we obtain *'I prefer'*:

gwell yw ganso neuvya	*He prefers to swim*
gwell via genev y weles a-vorow	*I would prefer to see him tomorrow*